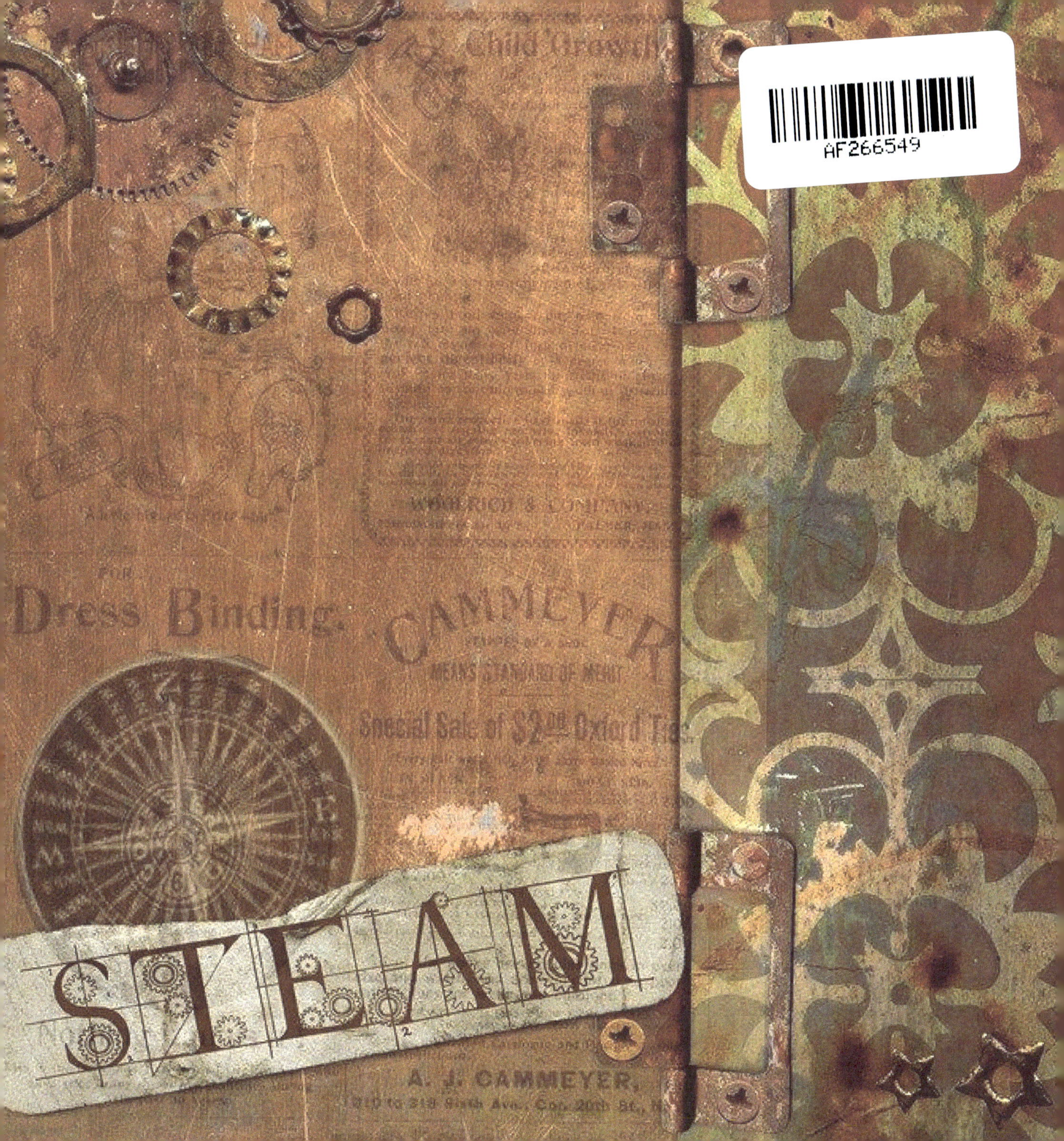
Child Growth
Dress Binding.
WOOLRICH & COMPANY
CAMMEYER
MEANS STANDARD OF MERIT
Special Sale of $2.00 Oxford Ties
STEAM
A. J. CAMMEYER,
AF266549

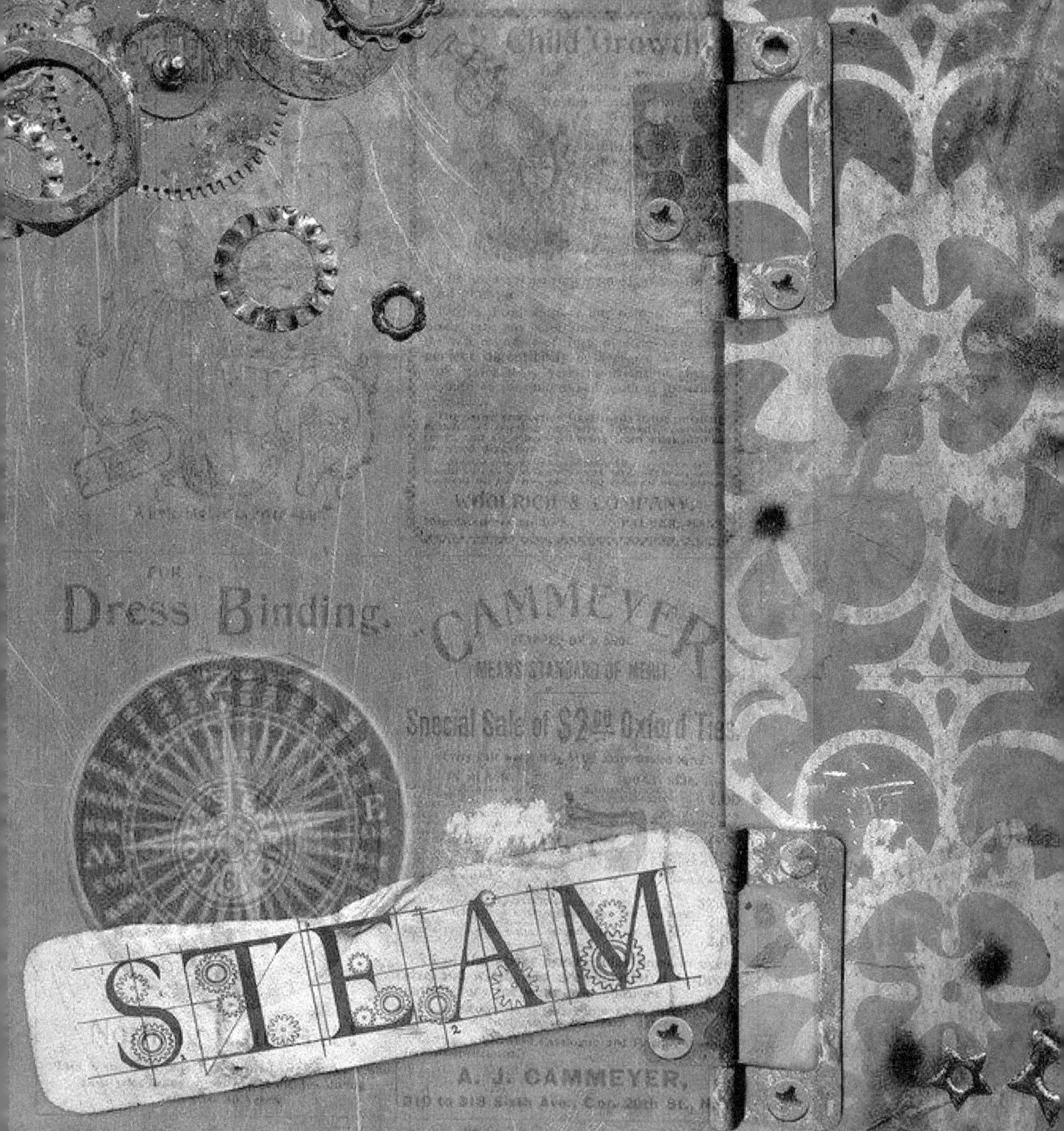
Child Growth
Dress Binding.
CAMMEYER
MEANS STANDARD OF MERIT
Special Sale of $2.00 Oxford Ties
STEAM
A. J. CAMMEYER,

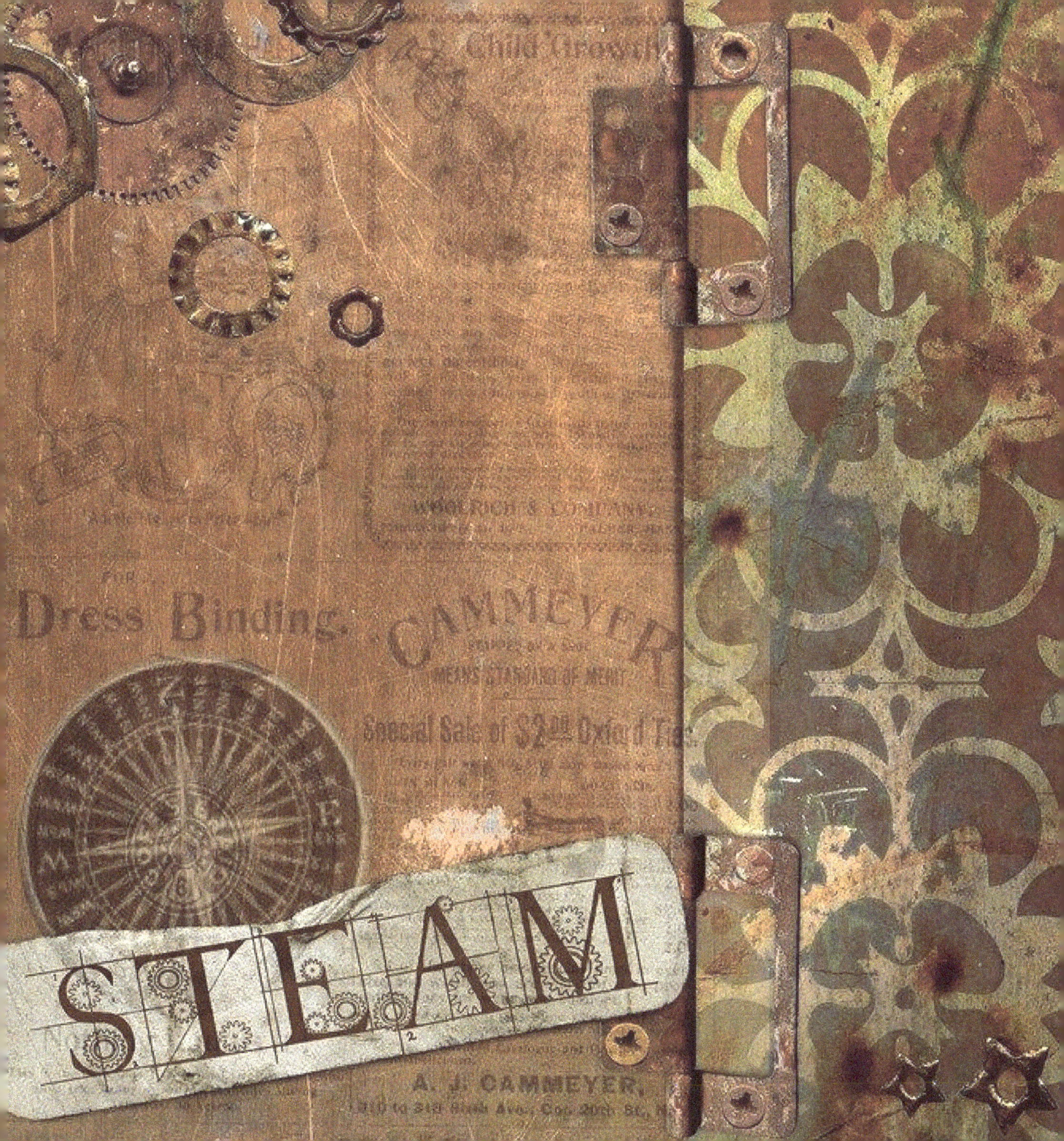
Child Growth
WOOLRICH & COMPANY
Dress Binding.
CAMMEYER
MEANS STANDARD OF MERIT
Special Sale of $2.00 Oxford Ties
STEAM
A. J. CAMMEYER,

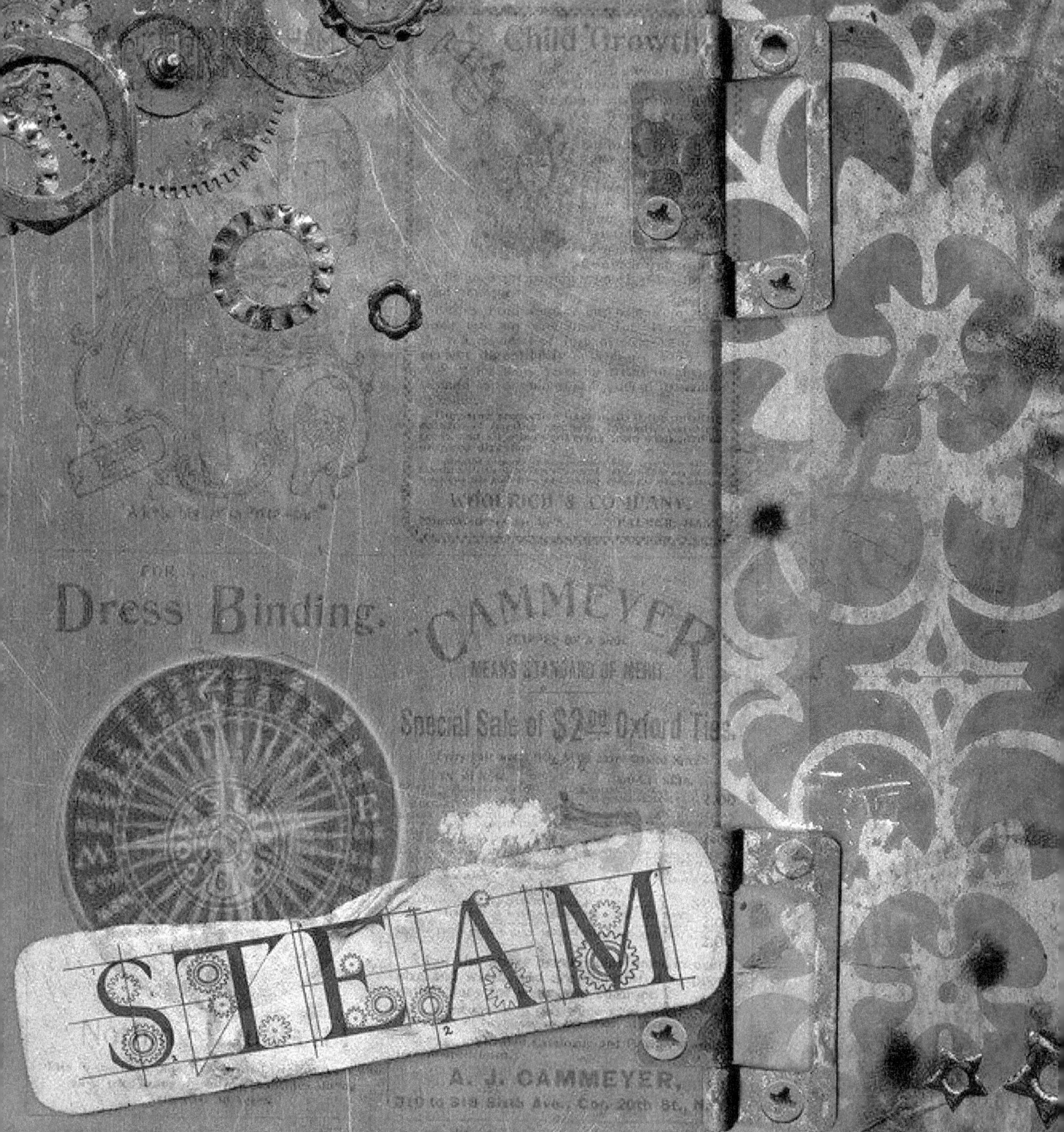

Child Growth
WOOLRICH & COMPANY
Dress Binding.
CAMMEYER
MEANS STANDARD OF MERIT
Special Sale of $2.00 Oxford Ties
STEAM
A. J. CAMMEYER,

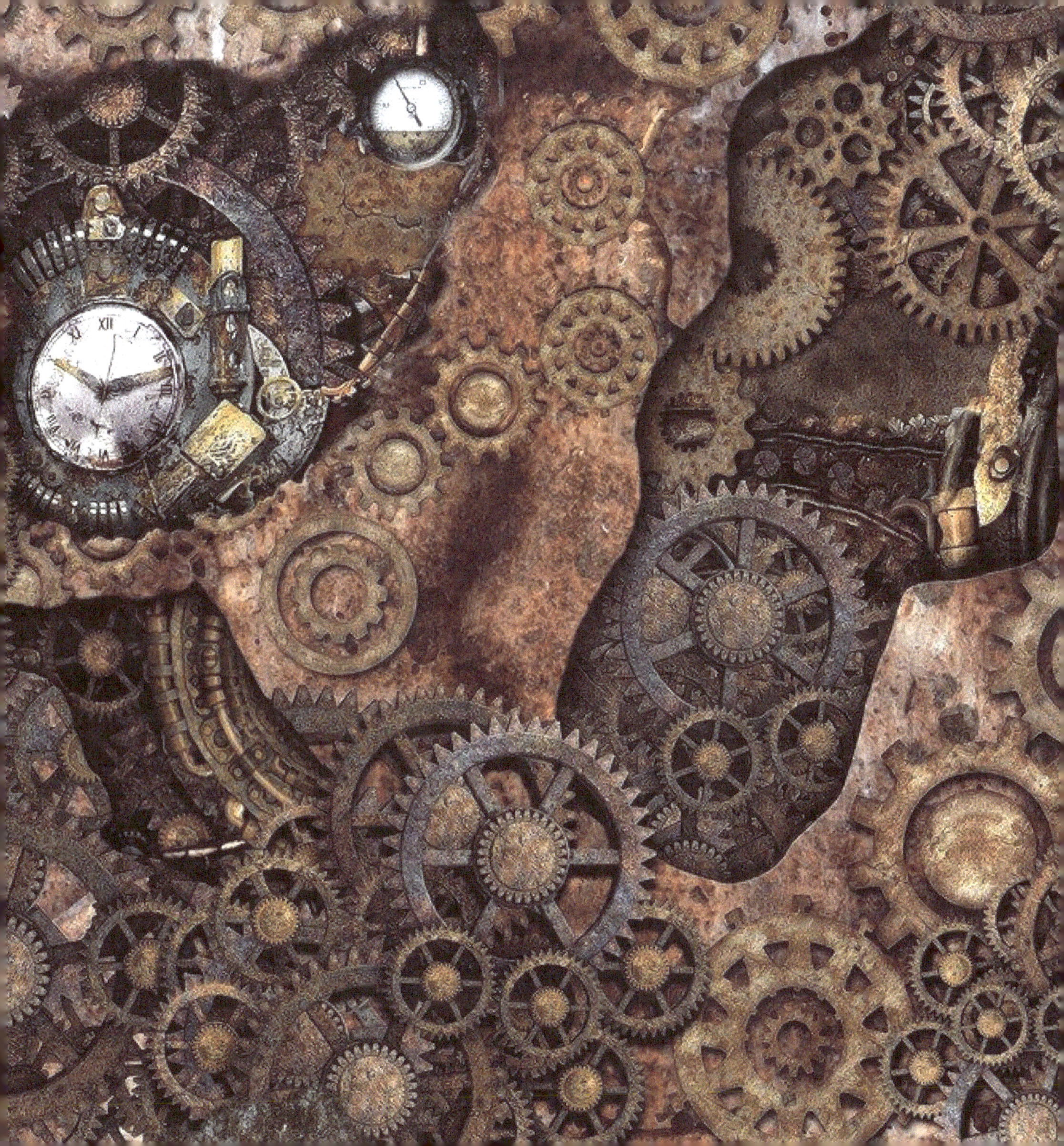

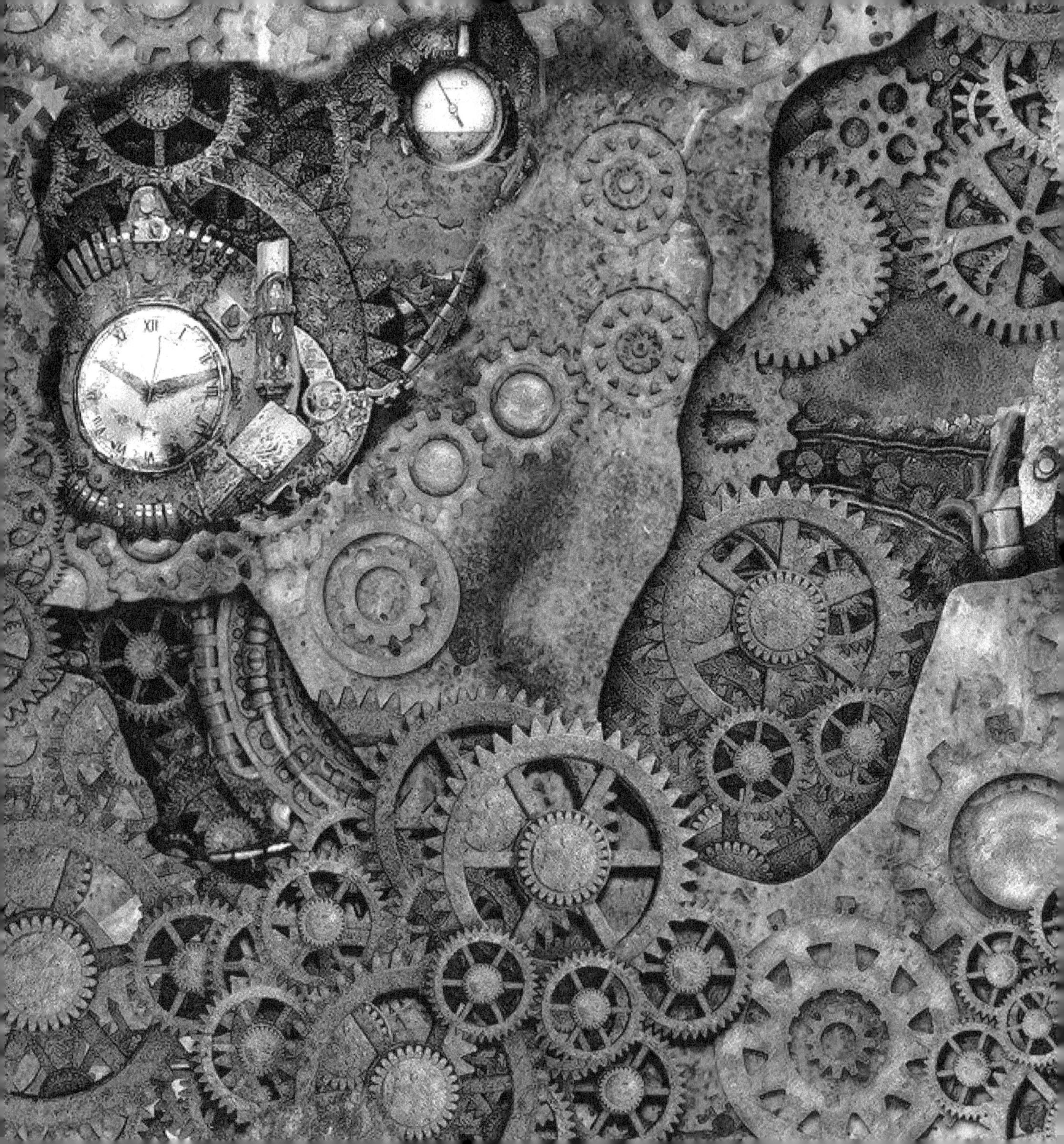

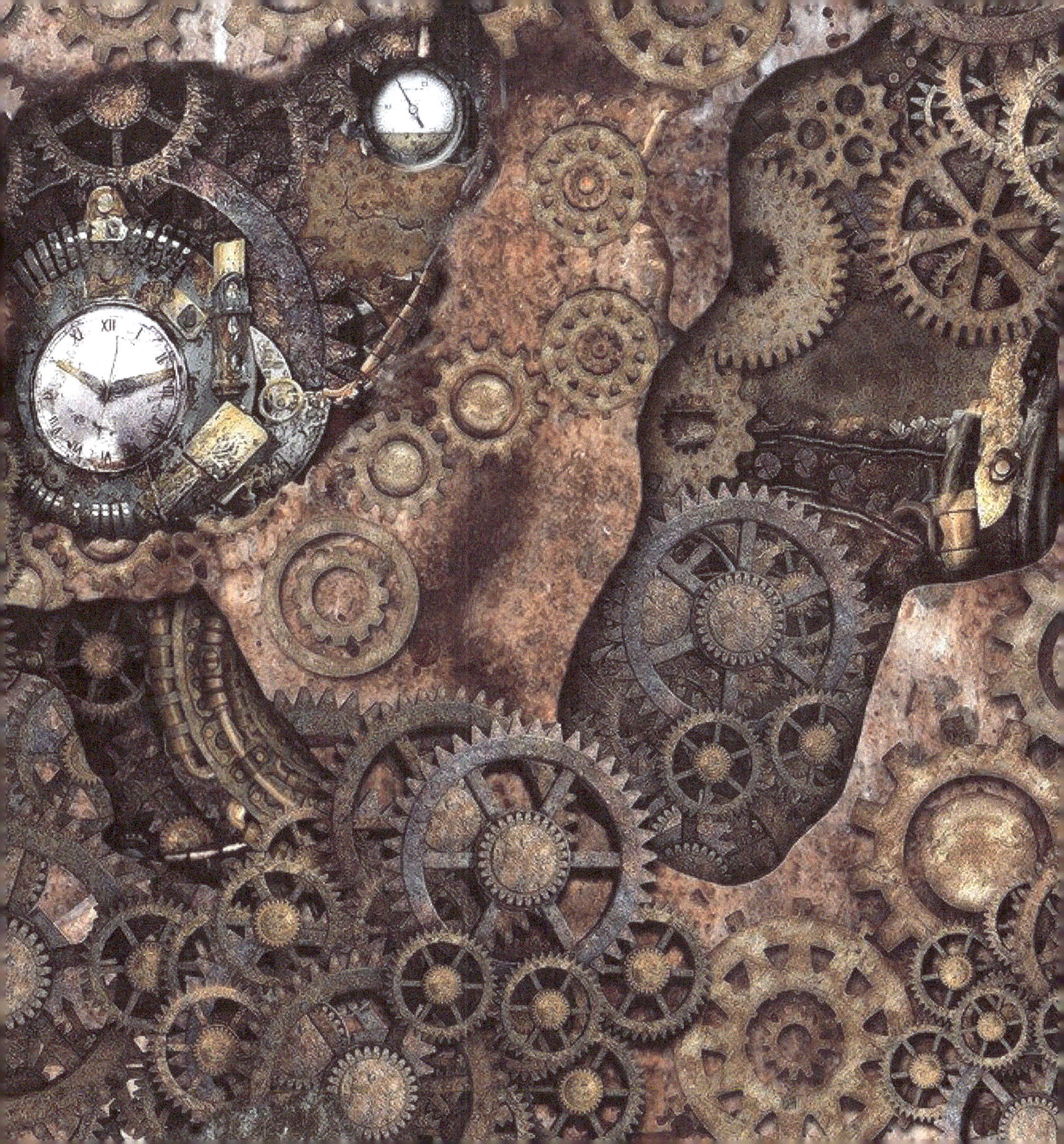

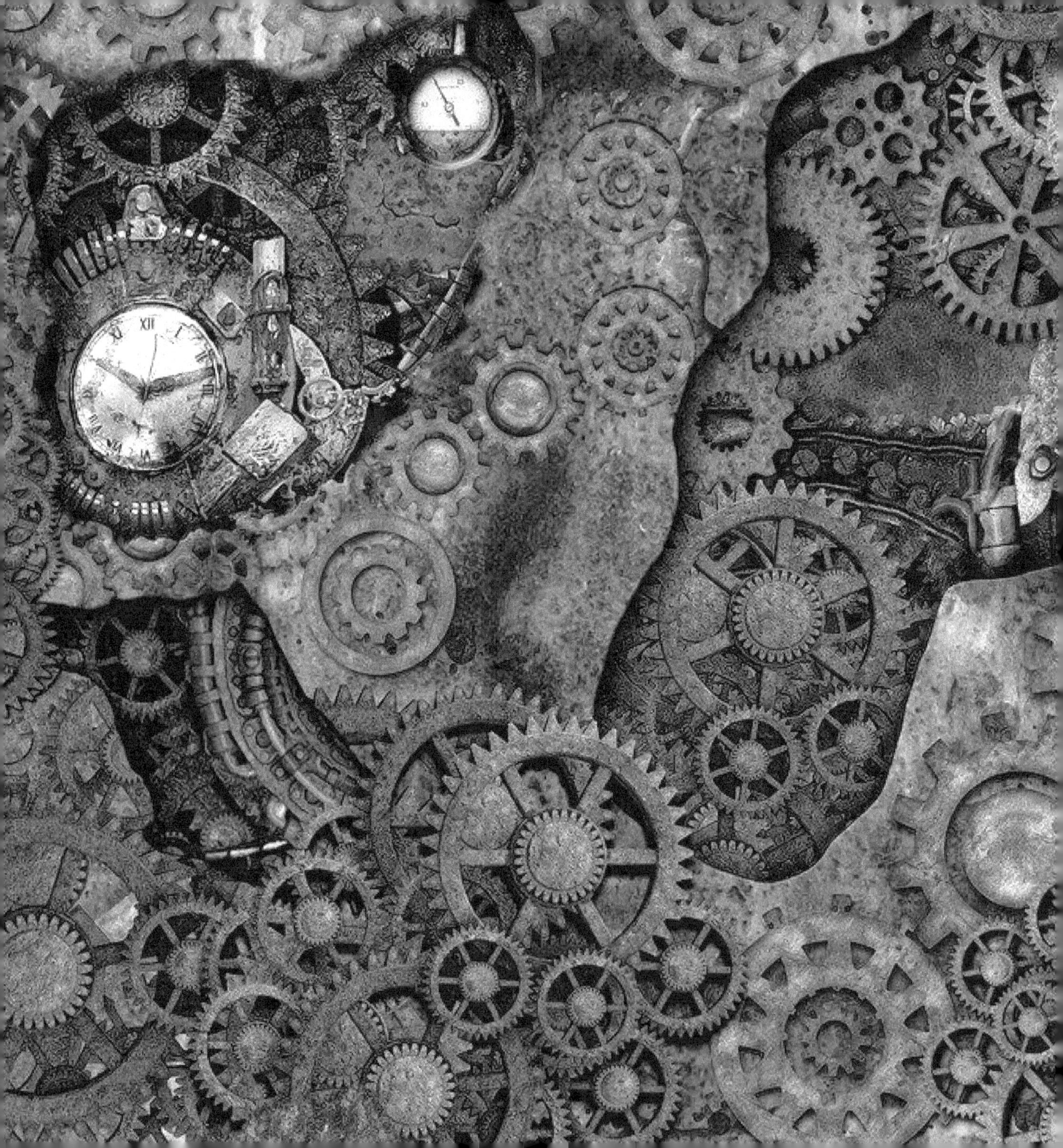

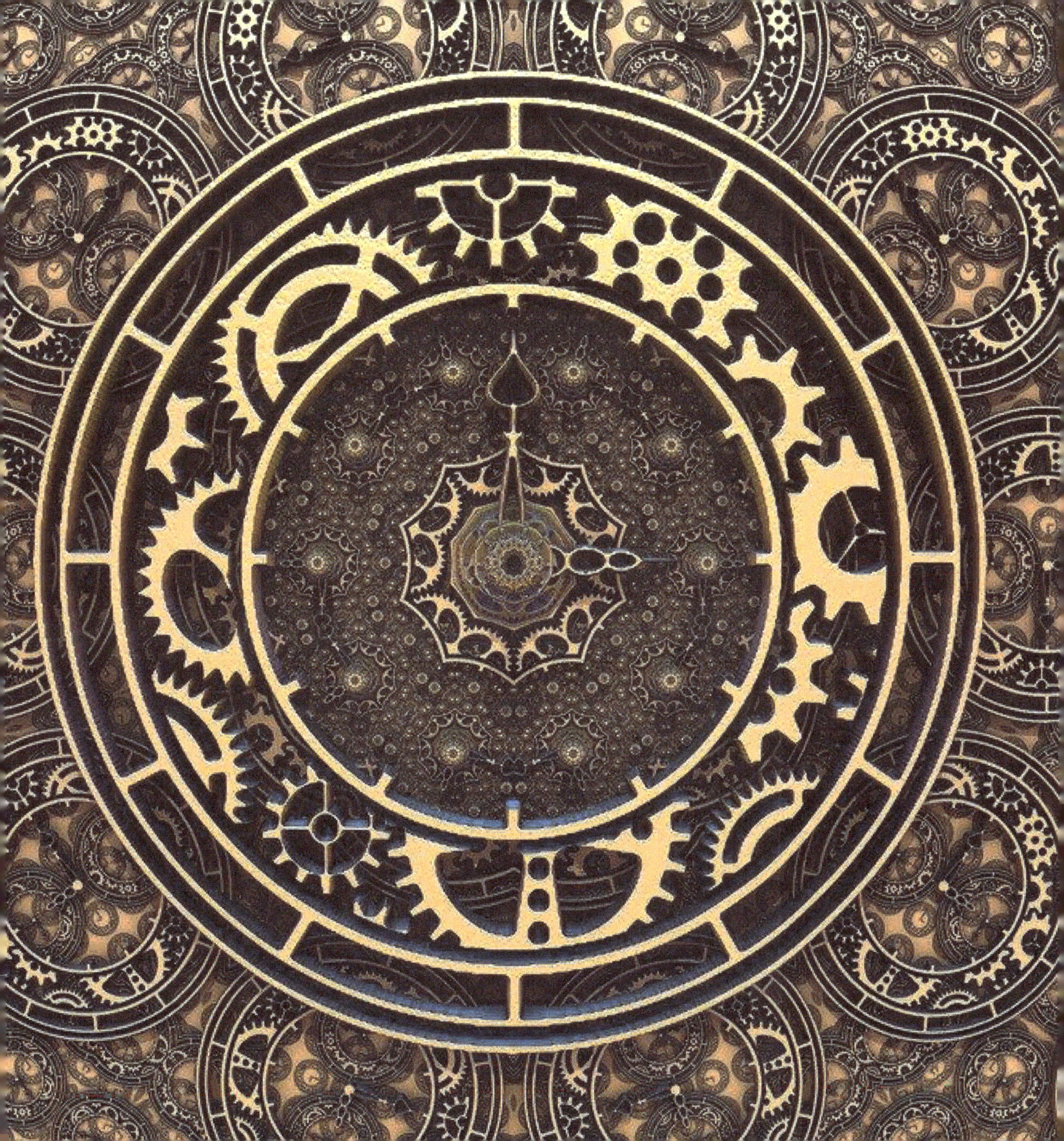

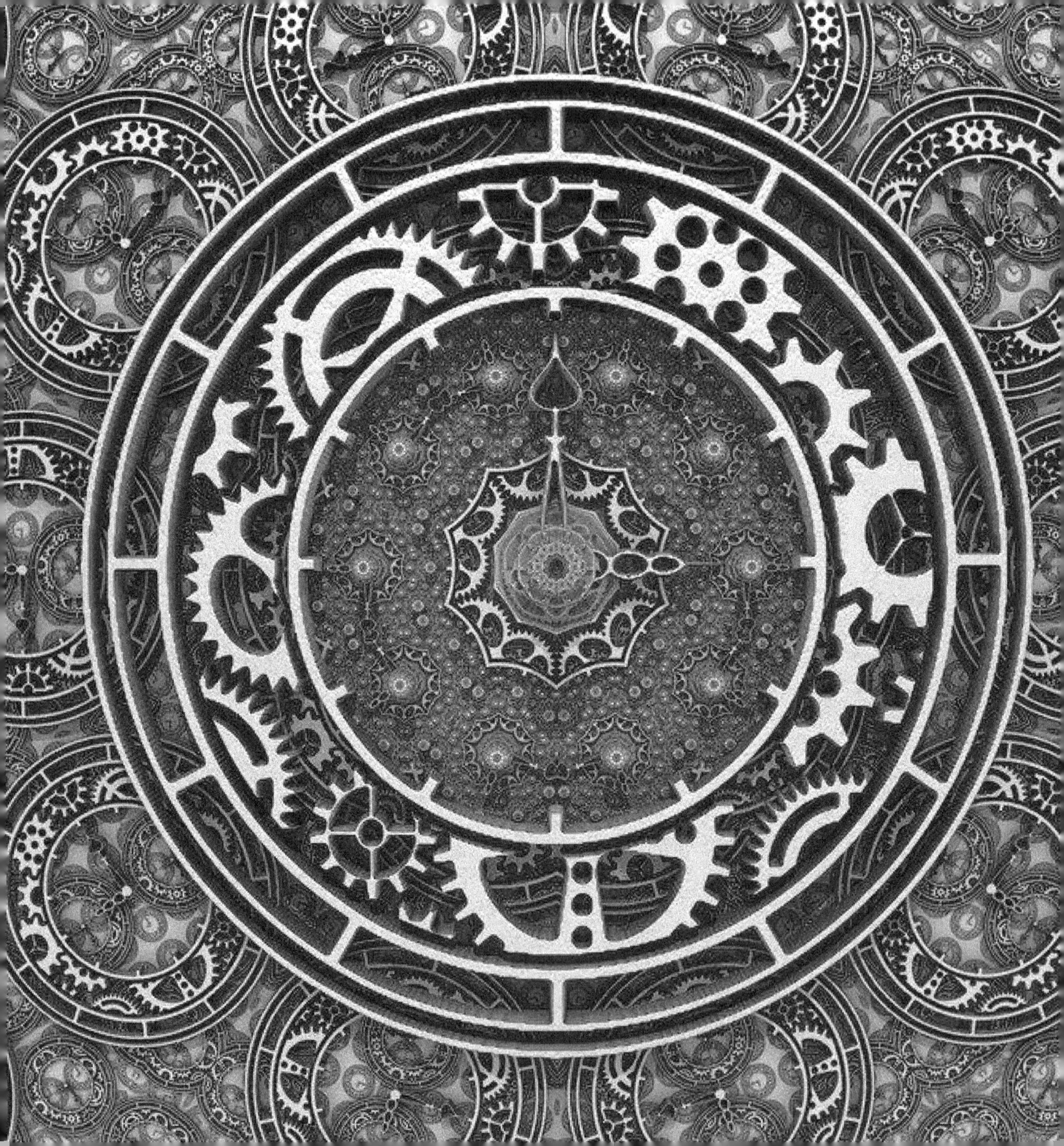

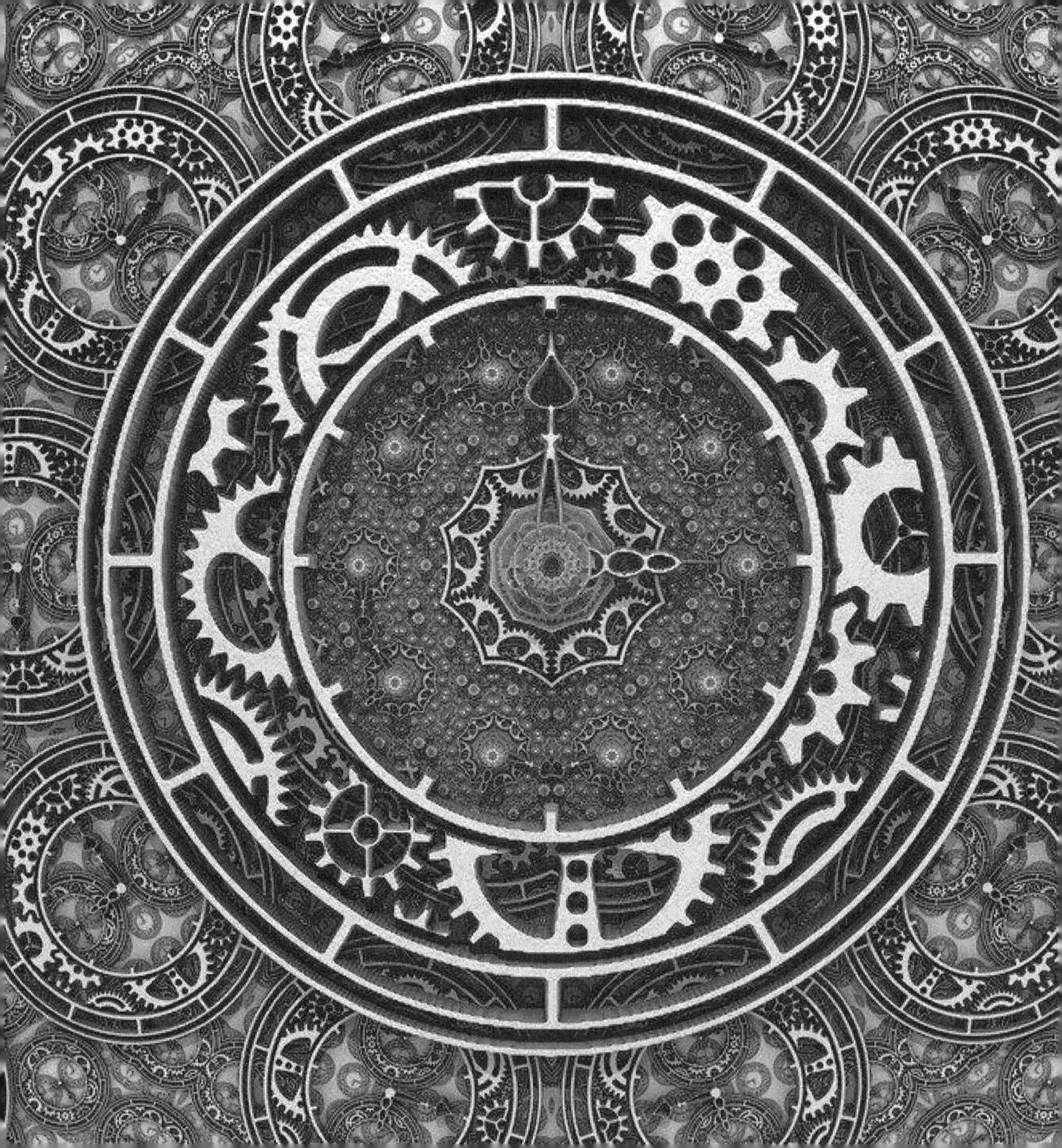

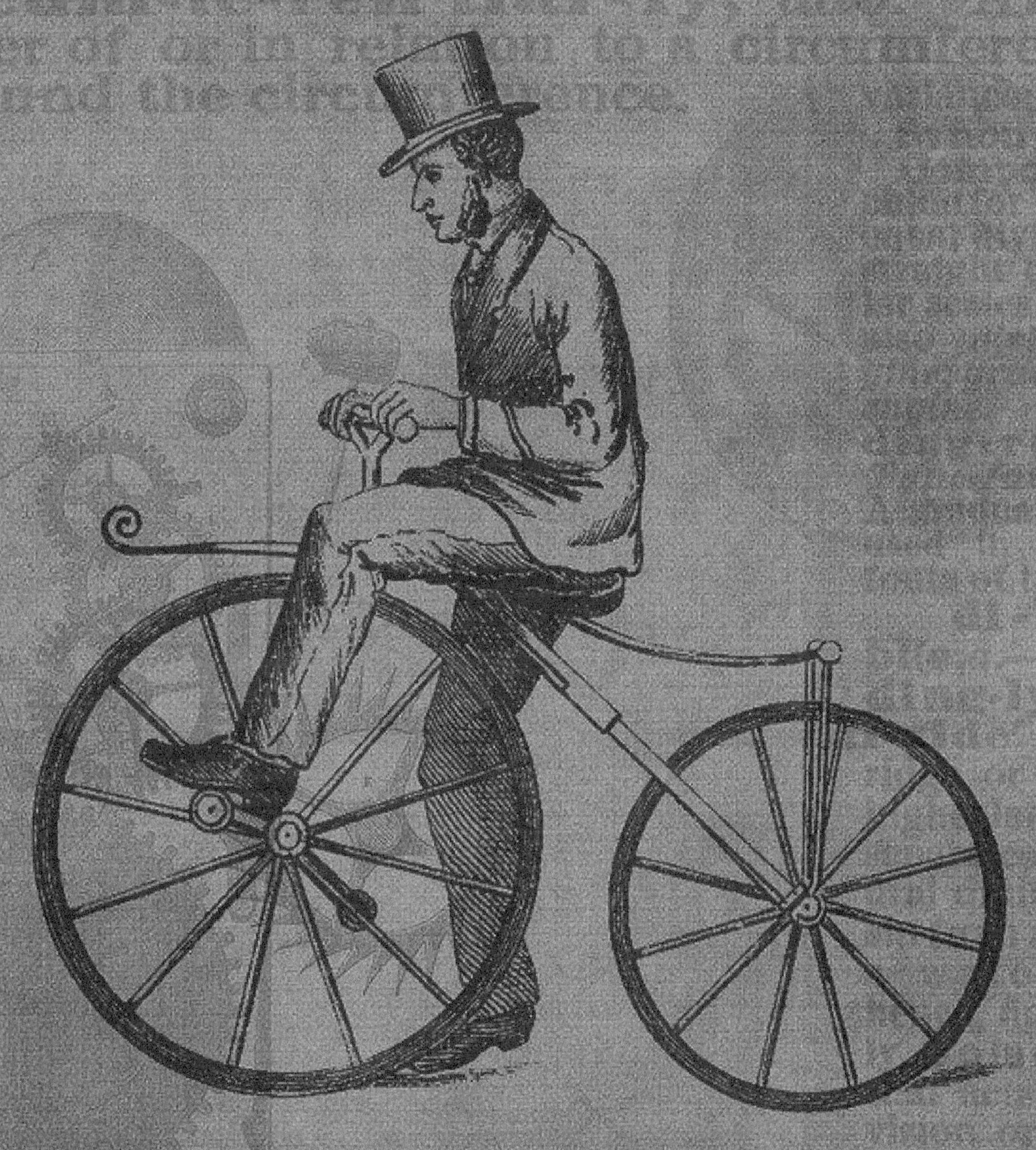

6 The "Bone-shaker."

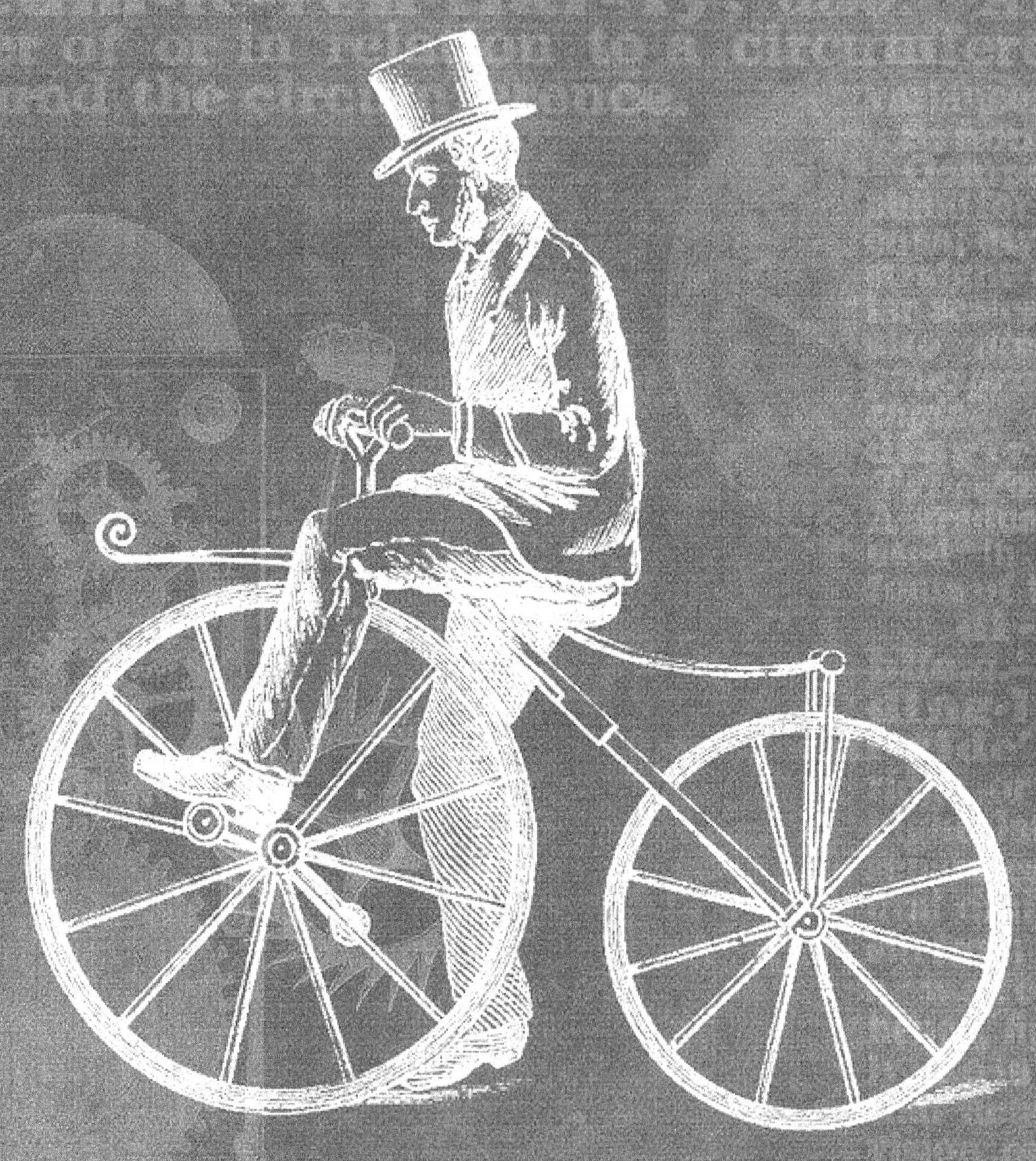

6 The "Bone-shaker."

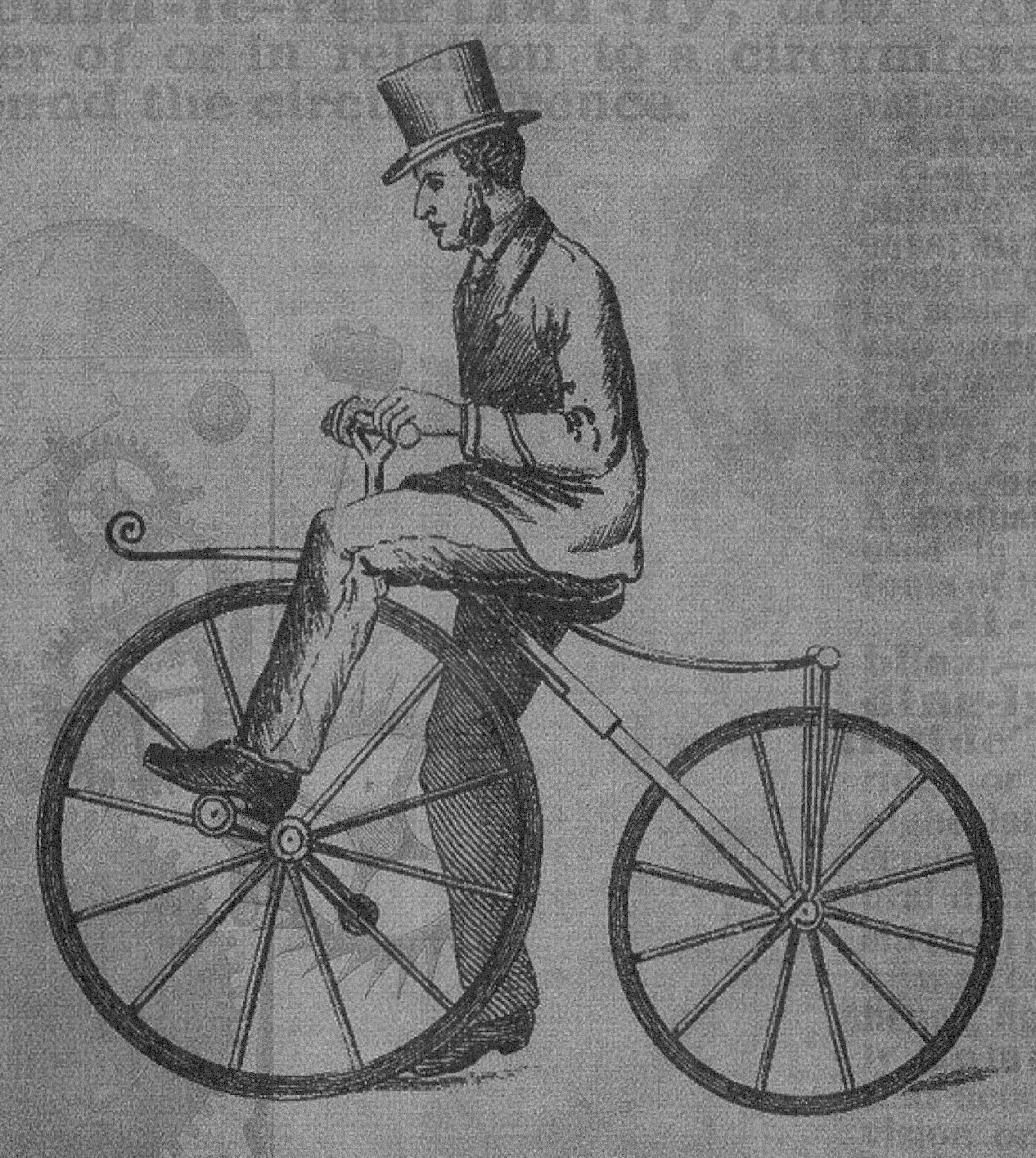

6 The "Bone-shaker."

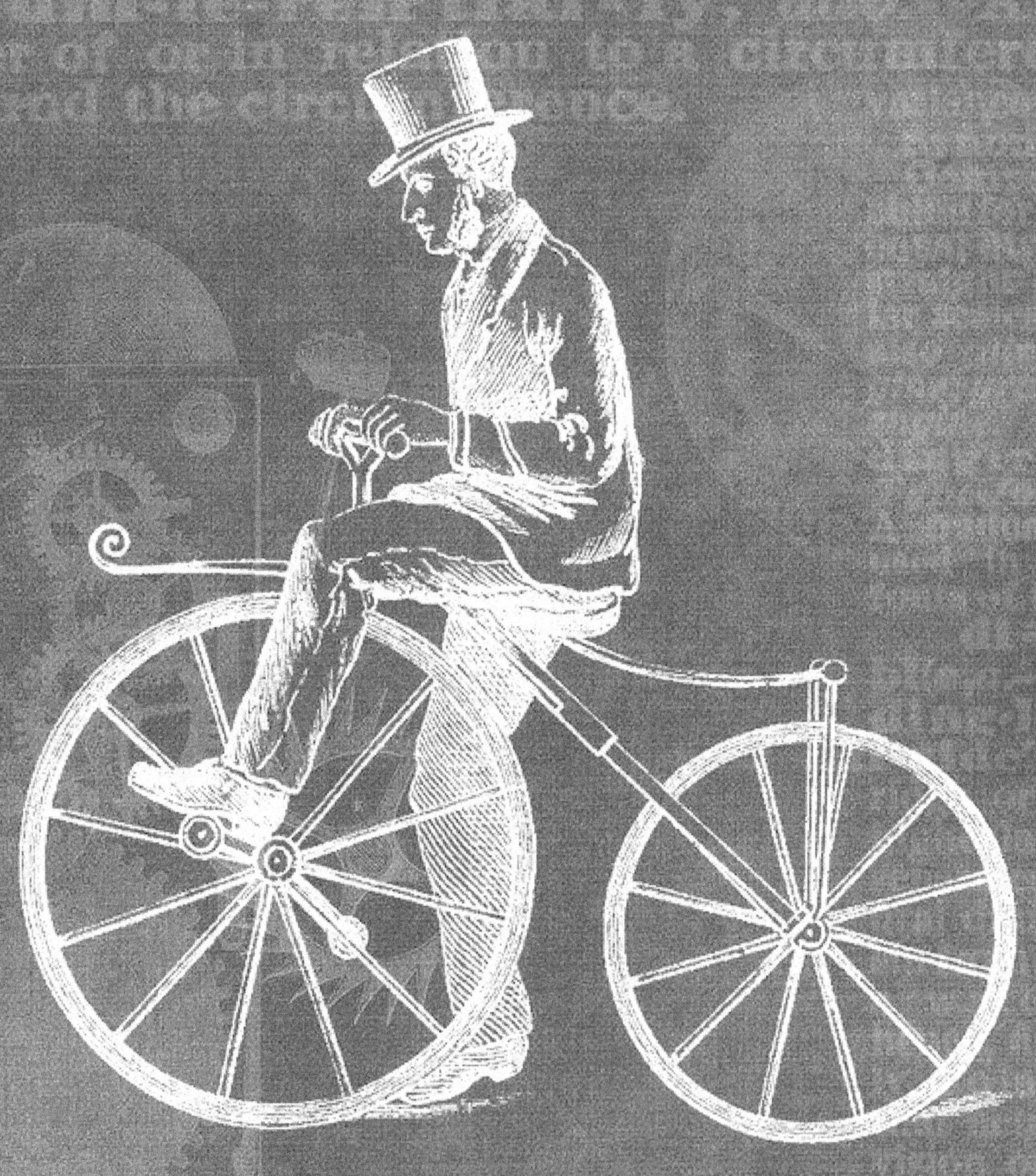

6 The "Bone - shaker."

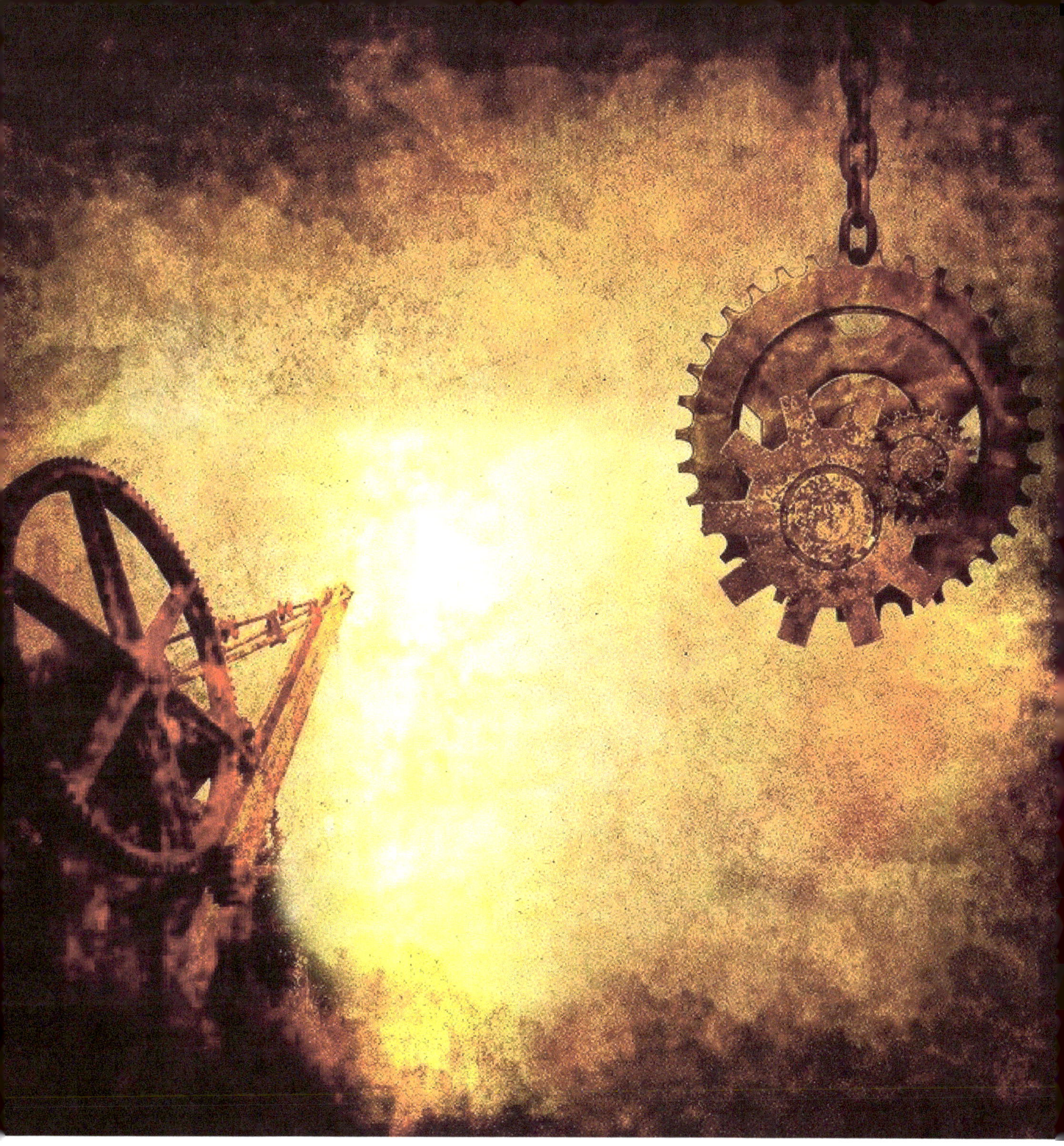

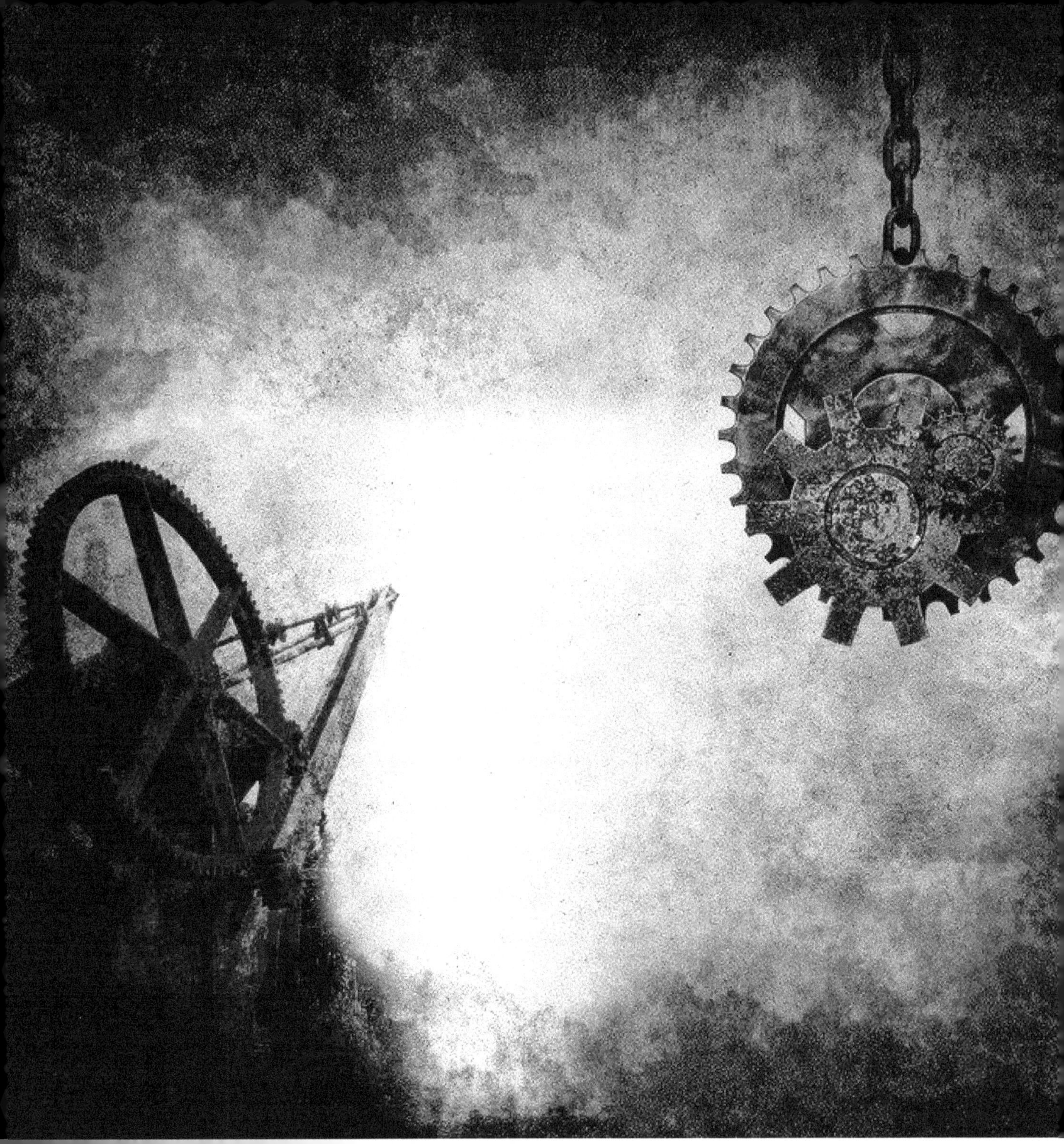

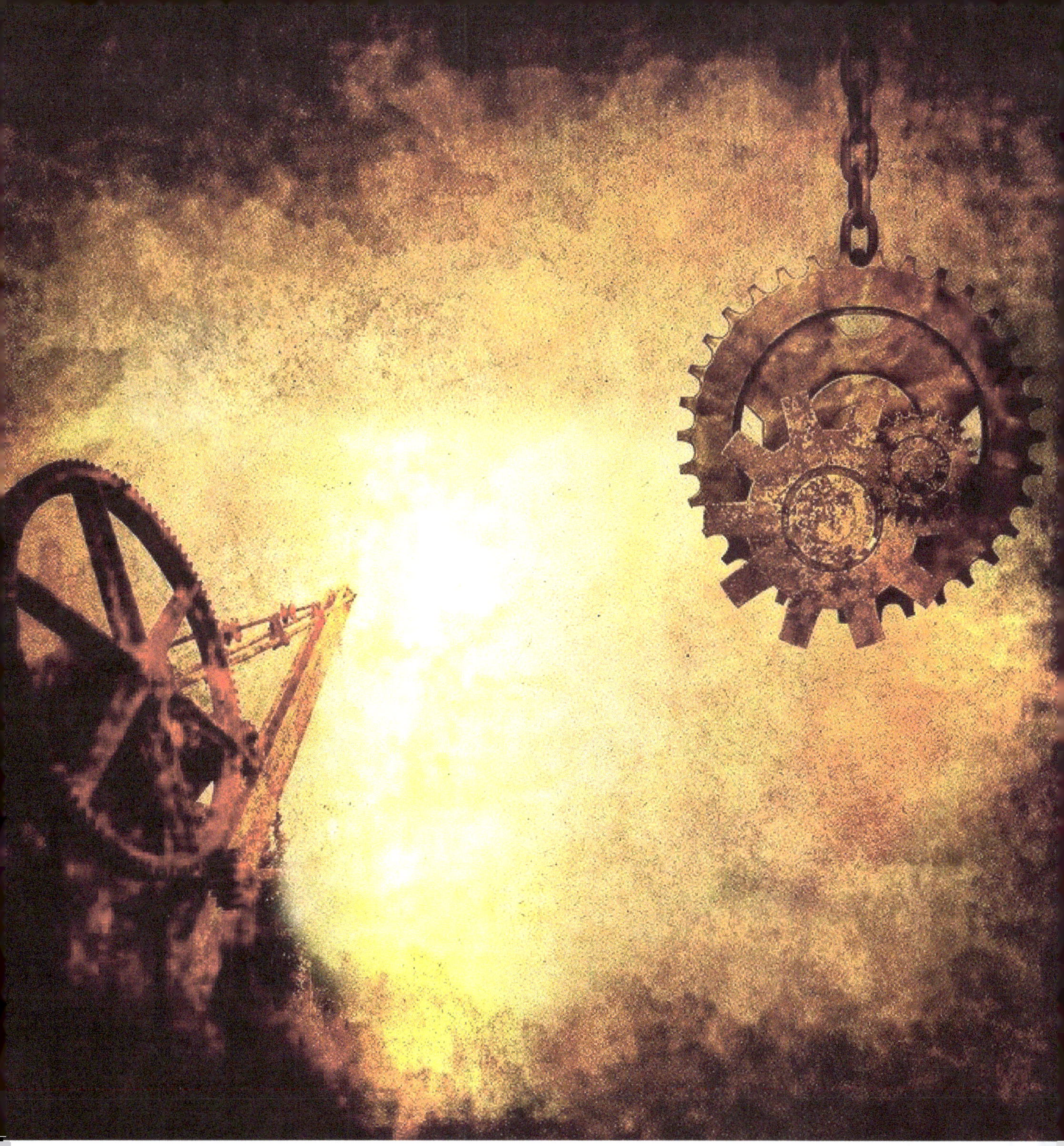

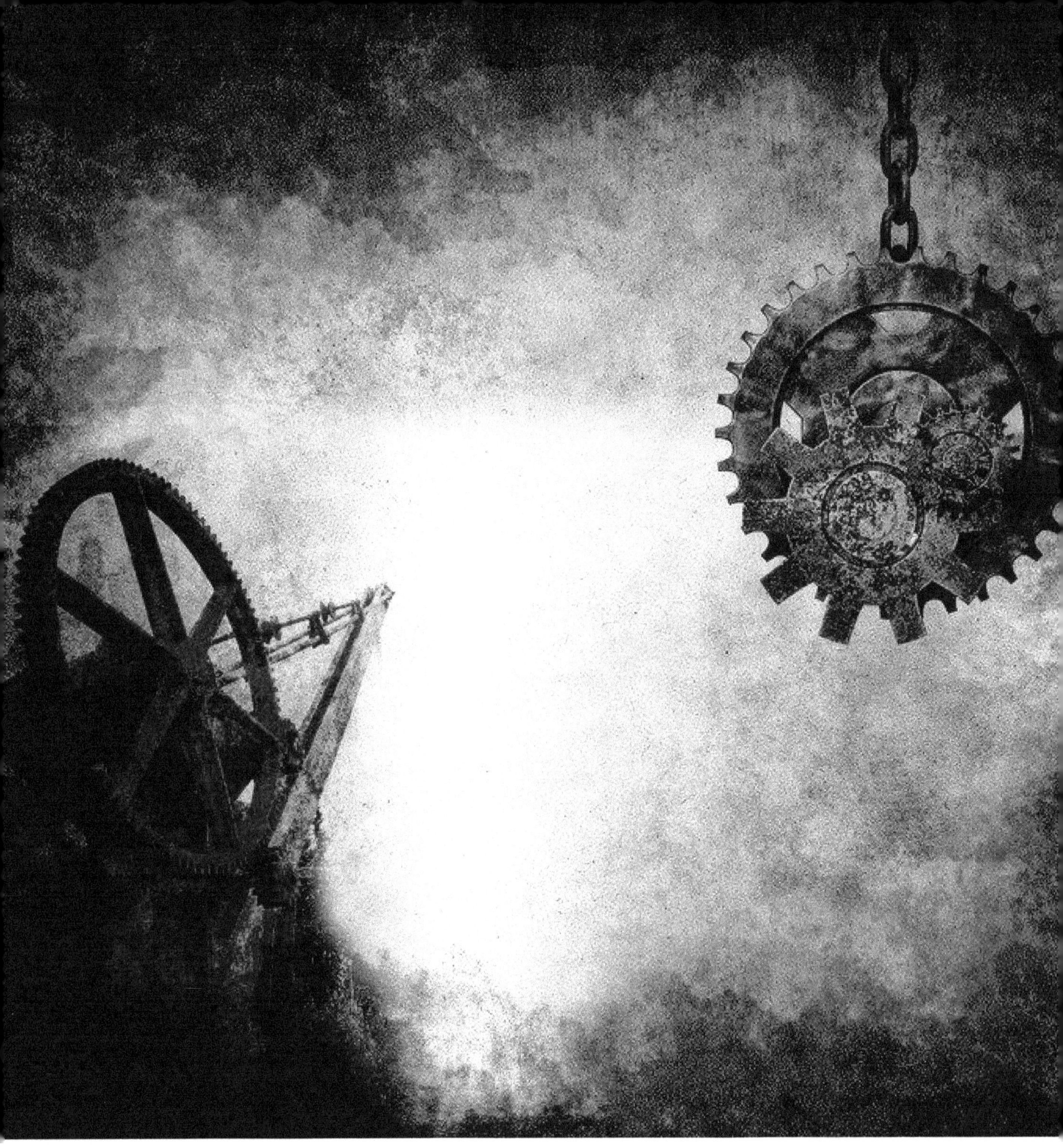

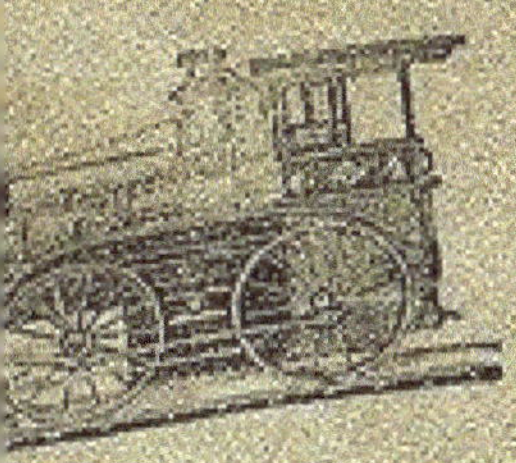

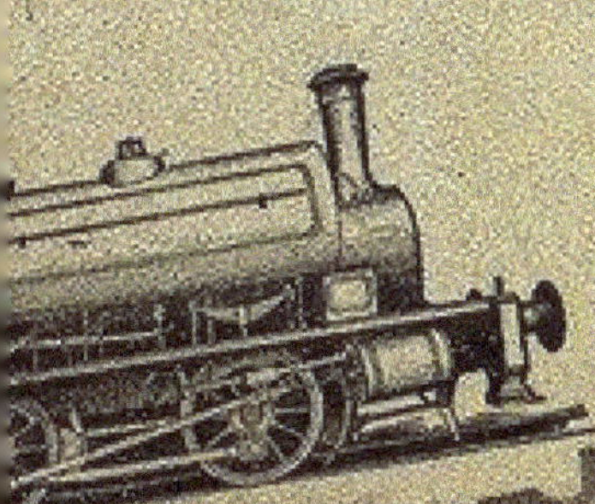

For these reasons, in my description of the evolution of the locomotive (and, indeed, of the machinery department generally), I shall strive to describe as nearly as I can the facts merely, without occupying too much space over unimportant details of place, and without straining to determine to whom the fact first became apparent.

In this connection I will mention, what young men may not know, that the practice of designating particular engines by specific names was

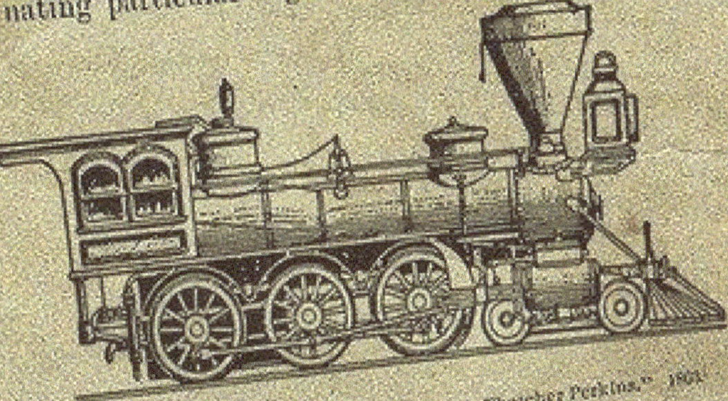

First Ten-Wheeled Passenger Engine. "Thatcher Perkins," 1863.

followed in the early history of railroads. This has now given place to the use of numbers. Proceeding to details, let us first take up the cylinder. Surely there is nothing about the machine of greater importance than this.

CYLINDERS.—The first locomotive designed by Trevithick, in 1803, had but one cylinder, placed horizontally on the inside. Up to 1826 the cylinders were placed vertically, half within the boiler. In 1826, when the engine "Experiment" was designed by George Stephenson for use on the Stockton and Darlington Railway, inclined

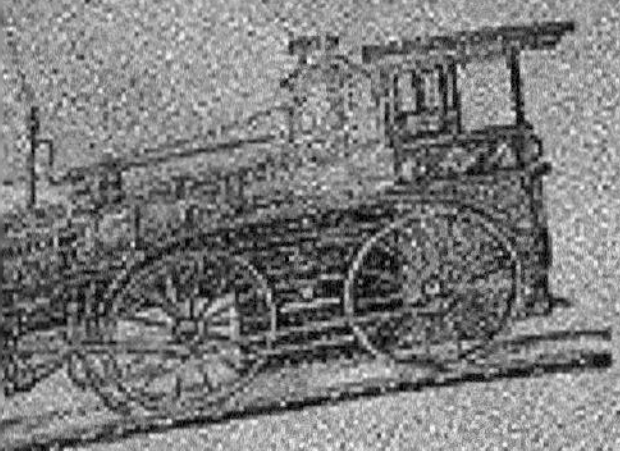

For these reasons, in my description of the evolution of the locomotive (and, indeed, of the machinery department generally), I shall strive to describe as nearly as I can the facts merely, without occupying too much space over unimportant details of place, and without straining to determine to whom the fact first became apparent.

In this connection I will mention, what young men may not know, that the practice of designating particular engines by specific names was

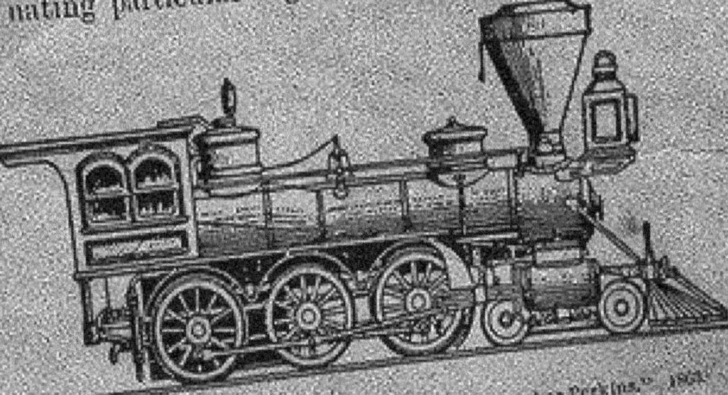

First Ten-Wheeled Passenger Engine. "Thatcher Perkins." 1863

followed in the early history of railroads. This has now given place to the use of numbers. Proceeding to details, let us first take up the cylinder. Surely there is nothing about the machine of greater importance than this.

CYLINDERS.—The first locomotive designed by Trevithick, in 1803, had but one cylinder, placed horizontally on the inside. Up to 1826 the cylinders were placed vertically, half within the boiler. In 1826, when the engine "Experiment" was designed by George Stephenson for use on the Stockton and Darlington Railway, inclined

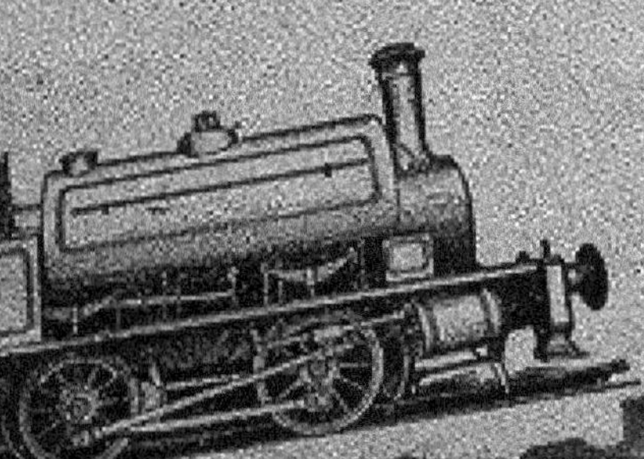

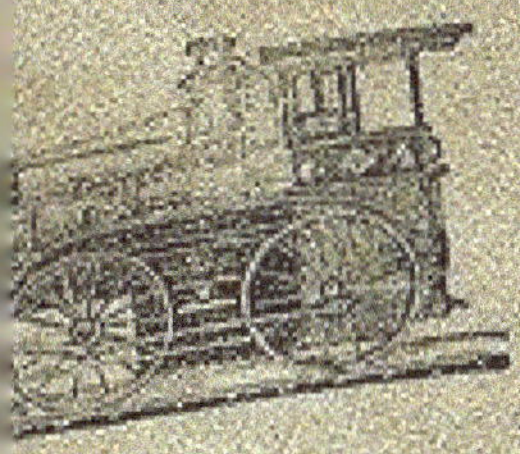

For these reasons, in my description of the evolution of the locomotive (and, indeed, of the machinery department generally), I shall strive to describe as nearly as I can the facts merely, without occupying too much space over unimportant details of place, and without straining to determine to whom the fact first became apparent.

In this connection I will mention, what young men may not know, that the practice of designating particular engines by specific names was

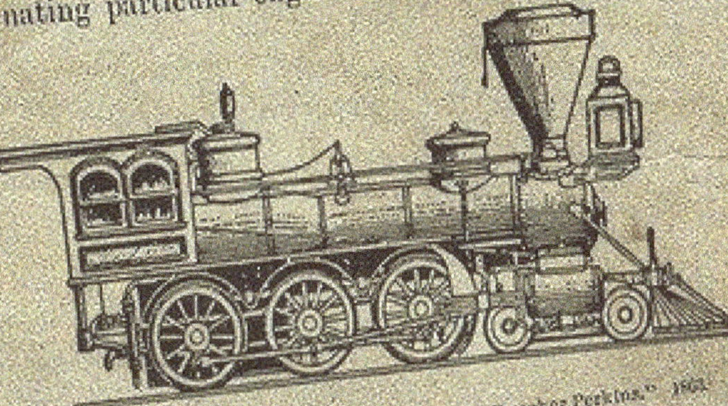

First Ten-Wheeled Passenger Engine. "Thatcher Perkins." 1863.

followed in the early history of railroads. This has now given place to the use of numbers. Proceeding to details, let us first take up the cylinder. Surely there is nothing about the machine of greater importance than this.

CYLINDERS.—The first locomotive designed by Trevithick, in 1803, had but one cylinder, placed horizontally on the inside. Up to 1826 the cylinders were placed vertically, half within the boiler. In 1826, when the engine "Experiment" was designed by George Stephenson for use on the Stockton and Darlington Railway, inclined

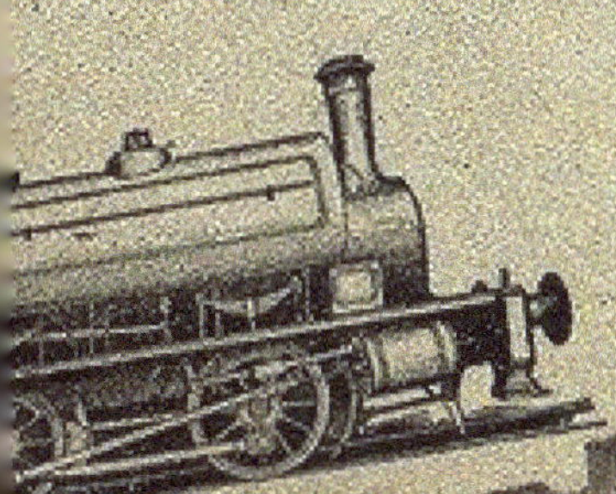

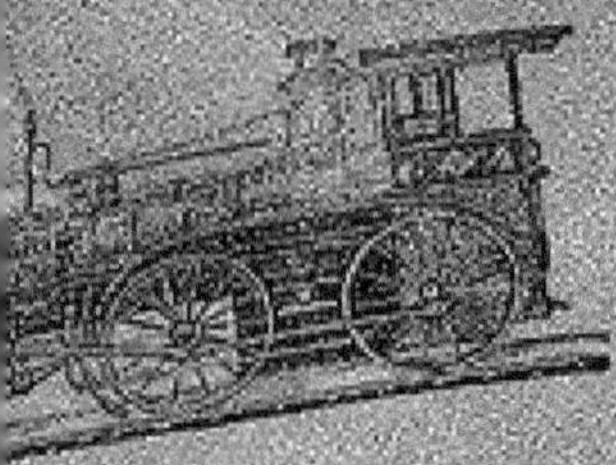

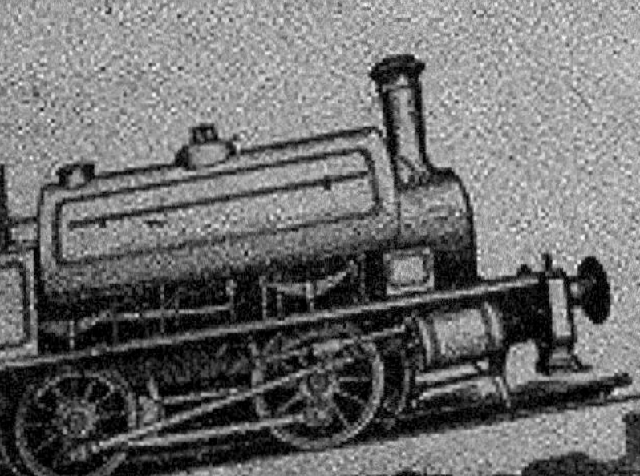

TIVE WORKS. For these reasons, in my description of the evolution of the locomotive (and, indeed, of the machinery department generally), I shall strive to describe as nearly as I can the facts merely, without occupying too much space over unimportant details of place, and without straining to determine to whom the fact first became apparent.

In this connection I will mention, what young men may not know, that the practice of designating particular engines by specific names was

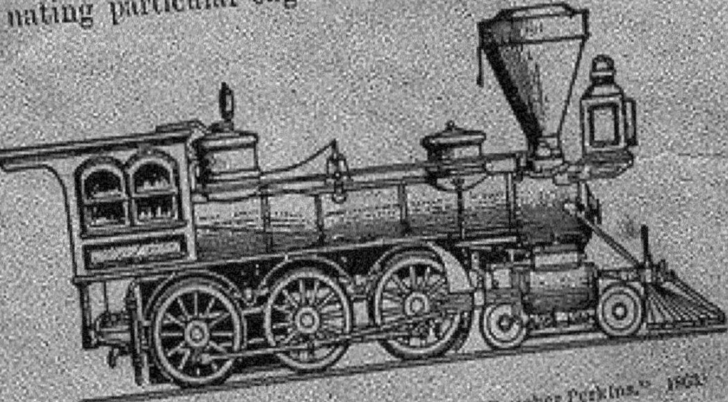

First Ten-Wheeled Passenger Engine, "Thatcher Perkins," 1863.

followed in the early history of railroads. This has now given place to the use of numbers. Proceeding to details, let us first take up the cylinder. Surely there is nothing about the machine of greater importance than this.

CYLINDERS.—The first locomotive designed by Trevithick, in 1803, had but one cylinder, placed horizontally on the inside. Up to 1826 the cylinders were placed vertically, half within the boiler. In 1826, when the engine "Experiment" was designed by George Stephenson for use on the Stockton and Darlington Railway, inclined